Other books by E. Perry Good

In Pursuit of Happiness

It's OK to Be the Boss

Helping Kids Help Themselves

by
E. Perry Good

Designed and Illustrated by
Jeffrey Hale

New View Publications
Chapel Hill

Fifth Printing, 1997

Design and illustrations by Jeffrey Hale

Library of Congress, Cataloging-in-Publication Data
Good, E. Perry, 1943-
    Helping kids help themselves / E. Perry Good; designed and illustrated
by Jeffrey Hale.
    p. cm.
    ISBN 0-944337-08-2 : $12.00
    I. Parent and child. 2. Child rearing. 3. Control theory.
4. Reality Therapy. I. Title
HQ755.85.G66   1992
649'.1—cd20   92-17485
                                                                    CIP

Author Speaking Engagements

For information regarding speadking engagements by E. Perry Good, contact the author at P.O. Box 3021, Chapel Hill, NC 27515-3021 or phone 919-942-8491.

Quantity Purchases

Companies, professional groups, clubs, and other organizations may qualify for special terms when ordering quantities of this title. For information contact the Sales Department, New View Publications, P.O. Box 3021, Chapel Hill, NC 27515-3021.

Excerpt of *The Seven Habits of Highly Effective People*, Stephen R. Covey, © 1989, Simon and Schuster. Used with permission of Covey Leadership Center, 3507 N. University Ave. Ste. 100, Provo, UT 84604.

Excerpt of *Getting Together: Building Relationships As We Negotiate*, Roger Fisher and Scott Brown, © 1988, Houghton Mifflin. Used with permission.

Manufactured in the United States of America.

DEDICATION

This book is for my daughter, Jessica, and for her three best friends, Erin, Kate, and Candice. Along with our wonderful Slovenian "son," Luka, these teens have helped me understand what helps and what does not.

Thanks to each of you.

A brief note on the word *KID*

Yes, the traditional definition of *kid* is "a young goat," but the word is quickly gaining acceptance as a synonym for child, youngster, or teenager. It's short, to the point, and sounds fun (which is what kids are)! I've asked kids (the humans, not the goats) and they prefer the term. This book refers to anyone between the ages of 3 and 21 as a kid. I have also alternated using the pronouns she and he for the sake of simplicity.

SPECIAL ACKNOWLEDGEMENTS

To Dr. William Glasser and his book *The Quality School*. Without either, this book would not exist. Thanks to Naomi and Bill Glasser for being there for me over the last twenty years, although I can't believe it has been that long!

To Diane Chelsom Gossen for her work on restitution which helped me clarify my thinking, and to Barnes Boffey who first introduced me to the concept of "the person you want to be." Diane and Barnes are not only my colleagues, but also the best of friends.

SPECIAL THANKS

To Jeff Hale who worked non-stop for three months to produce this book in record time.

To Kelly Lojk who edited the book with tenacity, spunk, and humor. Her insight and the changes she suggested improved the book enormously.

To Kathy Goforth who worked with Jeff Hale to design the book—no easy job, as you'll see when you turn the pages.

To Zika Font, my partner at work, who suggested that I write this book, and encouraged me all the way.

To Fred Good, for his vision of New View Publications and what it could be.

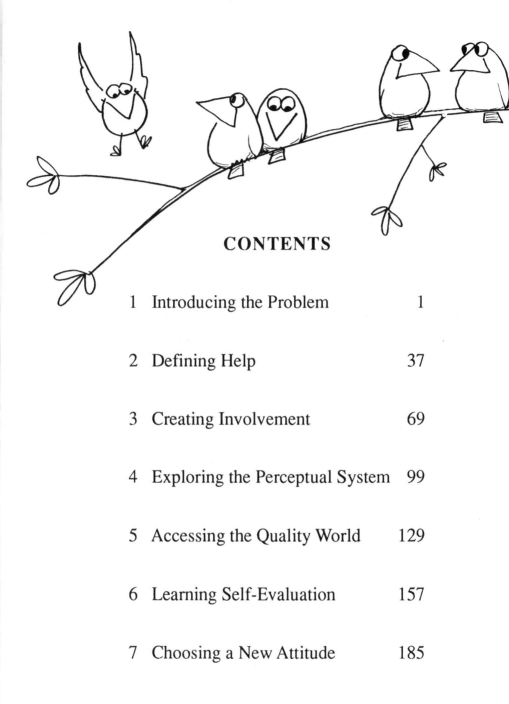

CONTENTS

1 Introducing the Problem   1

2 Defining Help   37

3 Creating Involvement   69

4 Exploring the Perceptual System   99

5 Accessing the Quality World   129

6 Learning Self-Evaluation   157

7 Choosing a New Attitude   185

"Of all the people you will ever know in a lifetime, you are the only person you will never leave or lose. To the questions of life, you are the only answer. To the problems in your life, you are the only solution."

Anon

INTRODUCING THE PROBLEM

There is no shortage of adults trying to help kids.

In fact, there are many more adults who want to help
kids ...

...than there are kids who want help.

GOOD INTENTIONS ARE NOT GOOD ENOUGH

Adults really do want to help kids, yet kids resist the "help" they are offered. Kids even cringe when they hear their parents say, "Let me give you some advice."

PERHAPS

teachers, counselors, and parents have a lot of faith in methods of "help" that do not work.

FREQUENTLY

the behaviors adults use to "help" kids don't help at all. What adults call help is many times a thinly disguised attempt to get the kid to do what the parent, teacher, or counselor thinks is best.

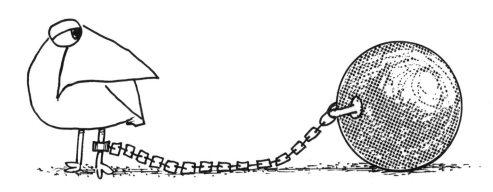

AND
SOMETIMES

the parent doesn't know WHAT to do to help. Unfortunately, we don't go to school to learn how to be good parents. The only instructors that a parent has previously had were his own parents and teachers.

ACTUALLY

the counselor thinks that telling the kid what to do will help. A counselor is very busy, and the quickest way to assist is to tell a kid what to do rather than to help the kid figure out what he wants.

AND
EVERY
NOW
AND
THEN

the teacher becomes frustrated and thinks that punishing her students will make them stop what they are doing and start doing what she wants them to do!

SO
WHAT

are some ineffective behaviors that adults use to try to help?

NAG

"When are you going to clean up your room? I've told you to do it five times already!"

PREACH

"You knew what was the right thing to do. Why didn't you do it? I'm ashamed of you."

GUILT

"After everything I have done for you, how could you?"

THREATEN

"If you don't stop talking immediately, I'm going to send you to the principal's office."

COMPARE

"I had your brother in my class last year. He is such a smart boy."

WORRY

"I just worry all the time because I don't think you are going to get accepted into a good college."

YELL

"Shut up!"

CRITICIZE

"You're really stupid. If you keep going the way you're going, I don't know where you'll end up."

HIT

"This hurts me worse than it hurts you, but next time I hope you will remember not to do that."

PUNISH

"Because you have done such a poor job in school, you won't be able to go out at all this weekend."

TAKE A LOOK

at your own "favorite" ineffective behaviors that you as a parent or teacher use to "help" your kids. Go ahead! You can't stop doing what you are doing that doesn't work until you know what it is that you ARE doing. For example, one of my favorite behaviors is nagging. I have a lot of faith in it even though I know that it doesn't work. On the next page, add your own favorite behaviors. Ask your kids what behaviors they see you using. You may be surprised at their answers!

YOUR TURN

What are some of the ineffective behaviors you use when you don't know what else to do?

WHY

DO ADULTS BELIEVE THAT THESE BEHAVIORS WILL WORK?

BECAUSE

our parents and teachers used these behaviors to "help" us. It is amazing that even though most adults know for a fact that these behaviors didn't help us, we continue to use them to try to get teenagers to do what we want them to do. On top of that, when these ineffective behaviors don't work, we simply up the ante and use more of them: yell louder, preach longer, give more advice, make the restriction longer.

ALL OF THIS BECAUSE WE

HOPE

SOMETHING WILL WORK

One of the reasons we think these behaviors will work is that sometimes they do, but only in the short run. They usually make the relationship with the kid worse. In the long run, they destroy the relationship and many times hurt the kid...

BECAUSE...these behaviors are

COERCIVE

Most of us have heard the word *coercion*, but it is not a regular part of our vocabulary. The majority of us are probably unaware that we coerce others daily.

THIS IS WEBSTER'S DEFINITION OF

COERCE

1. To restrain, control, or dominate, nullifying individual will or desire (as by force, power, violence, or intimidation).

2. To compel, to enact, or to choose by force, threat, or other pressure.

3. To effect, bring about, establish, or enforce by threat or other power.

The short definition of COERCE is to get someone to do what you want them to do (not what they necessarily want to do). The key word here is...

WANT

WHAT DO KIDS WANT

This is not a question that adults ask very readily. We want them to do what we want them to do, because we said to do it, we are the adults, and we know best. In an unscientific survey, I have found that many adults think that kids should just do what they are told and that what kids want is not important or in their best interest.

There are a few problems (to put it mildly) with taking the approach that kids should just do what they are told.

Many kids simply don't do what the adults in their lives ask, advise, or tell them to do.

This approach does not encourage kids to think for themselves, to learn how to make good decisions. The more we try to get kids to do what we want, the more likely we are to drive them into making foolish decisions just to prove that they can't be controlled by adults.

WHAT DO KIDS DO WHEN ADULTS COERCE THEM

THEY
ACT OUT

HERE ARE SOME OF THE
WAYS THAT KIDS ACT OUT

SCREAM

DESTROY

THREATEN

FIGHT

GET DRUNK

LIE

GET PREGNANT

WHAT **ELSE** DO

KIDS DO WHEN ADULTS
COERCE THEM

THEY

WITHDRAW

HERE ARE SOME OF THE WAYS
THAT KIDS WITHDRAW

SLEEP

LEAVE HOME

IGNORE

GET DEPRESSED

SULK

USE DRUGS

COMMIT SUICIDE

TAKE A LOOK

at some of the behaviors that you see your kids using at home or at school when they are coerced. Some behaviors I see my kid using are sulking, ignoring, and being sarcastic. On the next page, add some of the acting out or withdrawing behaviors that your kids use. Ask your kids to make a list with you. They know what they do!

YOUR TURN

DO IT

JUMP

YOUR TURN

How do your kids behave when they are coerced?

OBVIOUSLY...

no adult wants his kids to act out or withdraw. But these are exactly the behaviors we encourage when we coerce kids. The "helping" adult becomes just another brick in the wall.

The lyrics from a song by the rock group Pink Floyd seem to be as popular with kids today as when the song first came out in 1979.

"We don't need no education.
We don't need no thought control.
No dark sarcasm in the classroom.
Teacher, leave us kids alone...
All in all, you're just another brick in the wall."

Roger Waters

If we don't want to be another brick in the wall, if we are serious about wanting to help, what can we do that works?

DON'T DESPAIR

THERE
IS A
SOLUTION

DEFINING HELP

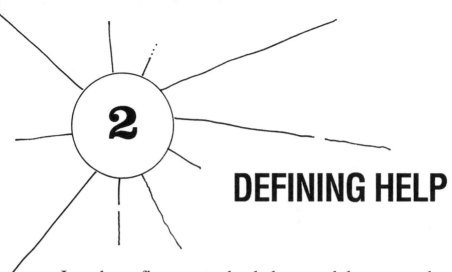

DEFINING HELP

In order to figure out what helps, as adults, we need to first think about what we really want. Ultimately, we want to help kids become…

RESPONSIBLE

INDEPENDENT

If this is our goal, then what do we do? What are effective, non-coercive behaviors that we can use? If we use these behaviors, is there a chance that we will actually HELP? Yes! We may not have kids who do exactly what we want, but we will have kids who are responsible and independent.

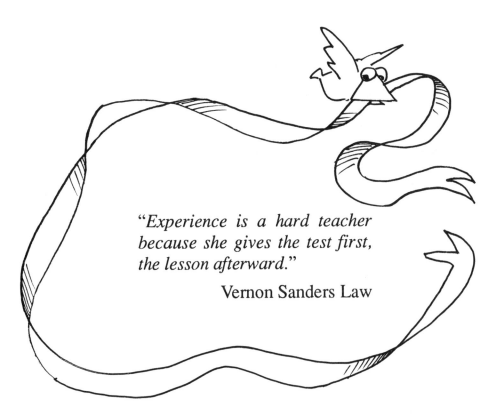

> *"Experience is a hard teacher because she gives the test first, the lesson afterward."*
>
> Vernon Sanders Law

Adults become major roadblocks to developing responsible and independent kids when they don't let kids experience life.

As adults, we want our kids to know about "things" without having to experience them. We have all been in situations that were painful and sometimes got us into trouble. Some adults think that shielding kids from unpleasant situations will help them. However, this is not so! For example, it is painful to a parent if his kid is arrested. But the "experience" of a few hours in jail might prevent his kid from being involved in an even worse situation.

Face it, your kids have to experience life in order to understand it. Your experience cannot replace theirs. This is a LIFE FACT!

MAKE A DECISION!

Do you as a parent, teacher, or counselor want to be a help or a hindrance on your kids' road to independence?

IF THE ANSWER IS A

HELP

READ ON

If the answer is a HINDRANCE, give this book away;
it will annoy you.

SO
WHAT CAN WE
DO TO HELP
KIDS BECOME
RESPONSIBLE
AND
INDEPENDENT

How do you manage kids? Management is something you do at the office, not at home or at school, right? WRONG! If we want to be effective with our kids, we can take the principles of good management and apply them in our homes and schools. The problem with managing others is that few people do it well. In a recent survey of American workers, over sixty percent said that they did not like their bosses. Most bosses, like many parents, teachers, and counselors, manage by using coercion. They get people to do what they want them to do without involving them in the decision making process.

These bosses are not lead-managers.

LEAD–MANAGERS USE EFFECTIVE, NON-COERCIVE BEHAVIORS.

WHAT DO LEAD-MANAGERS
DO DO DO DO DO DO DO DO

**INFORM
ENCOURAGE
RECOGNIZE**

45

INFORM

A lead-manager has all the knowledge needed to do a good job and she shares this information with the people she manages. In a sense, a lead-manager is a teacher. A teacher's job is not to force students to learn what they don't want to know, but rather to persuade students that what she knows will be helpful to them and that this information or knowledge will increase the quality of their lives. In other words, a REAL teacher helps students get what they WANT.

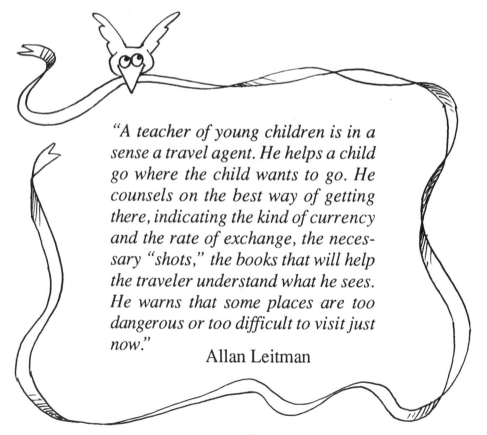

"A teacher of young children is in a sense a travel agent. He helps a child go where the child wants to go. He counsels on the best way of getting there, indicating the kind of currency and the rate of exchange, the necessary "shots," the books that will help the traveler understand what he sees. He warns that some places are too dangerous or too difficult to visit just now."

Allan Leitman

Many kids do not see their parents as teachers—for good reasons. One GOOD REASON is that many parents are not willing to teach what their kids really want to know.

Another reason is that kids are often embarrassed to ask their parents about things that really interest them. Kids have a lot of questions about subjects such as drugs and sex. Many times adults disapprove when kids inquire about these "controversial" subjects. Kids know when adults are uncomfortable with their questions, so they do not ask about them. It's even embarrassing to go with your parents to a movie that shows explicit sex scenes. (I've noticed that this phenomenon does not necessarily diminish with age.)

SO WHAT CAN ADULTS DO TO GET KIDS TO TALK TO THEM?

INFORM THEM ABOUT WHAT THEY WANT TO KNOW!

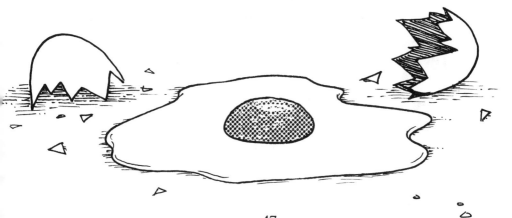

Do you remember on the TV show DRAGNET when Detective Friday used to say...

Detective Friday was really telling people to keep their opinions to themselves. This is hard to do, especially with your own children. However, you can share your opinions with them if (and this is a big if) you preface them by saying, "This is how I see it, but you will have to make up your own mind." A lot of times we don't want kids to make decisions on their own, we just want them to do what they are told. I am no exception. But if my kid always did exactly what I tell her to do, would she learn to think for herself? Would she learn to be independent and responsible? What about when I'm not there? Would she do what I tell her to do now, but rebel when she gets older (as often happens with kids)? If you want your kids to grow up to be responsible and independent thinkers, go ahead and tell your kids your opinions. Just don't force them down their throats. Let them come to their own conclusions.

Kids respect adults' opinions if we tell them how we arrived at them. As parents, teachers, and counselors, we are sometimes not willing to share that information. For example, a mother may be very opposed to teenage sex because she became pregnant as a teenager and it was a traumatic experience for her. However, what she might tell her kids is that she is opposed to teenage sex because of the great danger of getting AIDS. The reasoning she gives is certainly valid, but it is not the primary reason for her opinion. Kids will appreciate your being frank with them, so be

HONEST!

"Everybody is always telling us, 'You should be this. No, you should be that.' When they're not telling you one thing or another to your face, you still hear the voices in your head. I don't know if I'm the same or different from a lot of kids, but in my head all I hear are people's orders and suggestions and ideas. It's like the whole world is trying to put something into me. It makes me feel like a pincushion."

Teenager

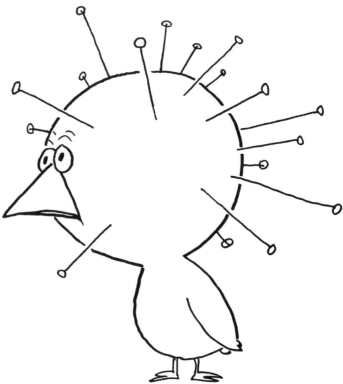

WHEN KIDS ARE LEARNING WHAT THEY WANT TO KNOW, THEY DON'T FEEL LIKE PINCUSHIONS.

TAKE A LOOK

at how often you give a kid some information she wants without the "editorial" comments. For example, a student asked me if it was really true that if you smoke cigarettes, you are certain to get lung cancer. Instead of preaching about the evils of smoking, I told her that smoking does not guarantee lung cancer, but it does greatly increase the risk of getting the disease. On the next page, think of situations in which you gave kids the information that they wanted without preaching or advising.

GO FOR IT

YOUR TURN

DON'T BE A CHICKEN

YOUR TURN

What are some examples of situations where you helped kids by informing them of "just the facts"?

ENCOURAGE

Most kids are doing the best they can in a very difficult situation. What is this situation?

GROWING UP

Growing up was never easy, and it's especially difficult now. Modern life is confusing enough for adults. Stop and think about what it must be like for kids today. They need all the encouragement they can get from the adults around them. Is this what they get? They get a lot of suggestions, advice, and opinions, but not much encouragement.

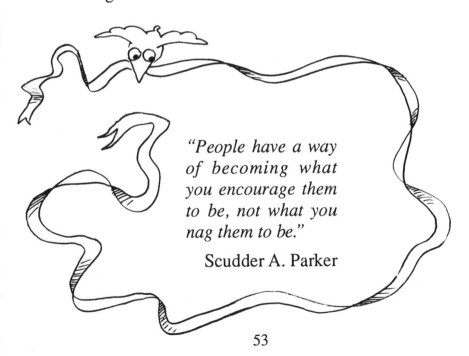

"People have a way of becoming what you encourage them to be, not what you nag them to be."

Scudder A. Parker

A FAN CLUB

I wish I had a fan club to cheer and yell and scream me on, after making a 44 on my language exam and spending detention in Mr. Anderson's office. I really need the praise.

Joey Reynolds
Junior High School Student

Instead of becoming a "fan club" to the kids with whom we are living or working, we end up becoming adversaries. Common sense tells us that it is stupid to have an adversarial relationship with either our own kids or our students. Yet, instead of encouraging them, we often put them down. Enemies are not created overnight. Nobody looks at a newborn baby and says, "What a disappointment." Nobody starts a career as a teacher saying, "I can't stand children." or "Children aren't what they used to be." Adversarial relationships between kids and adults build up slowly, one discouraging remark or negative experience at a time.

I once asked some high school kids what adults could do that would encourage them. One answer was that adults could LISTEN and pay attention to what they have to say.

Though adults may think they are listening, often they filter the information, hear what they want to hear, and ignore the rest. For example, a father might ask his daughter, "How was your basketball game?" His daughter replies, "We won, but I played terribly. I missed the basket nine times and it was really embarassing." Instead of talking to her about her embarrassment, the father tells her, "Oh, that's O.K. The team won; that's what's important."

Another answer struck me as sad, as evidence of how kids view their relationships with the adults around them...

"If adults don't put me down or push me back when I'm trying to go forward, I'll do alright."

What are some ways to encourage kids?

1 Send a note. (Yes, even to your own kid.) It may sound silly, but kids like to get encouraging notes from the adults in their lives. Sometimes they take what you have to say more seriously if you write it down. You could even have special cards you use just for encouraging notes. Here is a letter a mother sent to her daughter when she received a bad grade on her report card and was very upset.

> Dearest Daughter,
> I know you are discouraged by your report card. Please don't worry. You are making A+'s in everything your dad and I think is important in life! You are honest, responsible, and independent. You are also a truly nice human being. None of the rest _really_ matters.
>
> Hugs and kisses
> Mom

2 Give a small surprise which sends the message to keep up the good work or to keep trying. For example, a favorite meal, a special treat for dessert, or a small gift—it doesn't have to be much. All of us like pleasant surprises; they make life more fun.

3 Notice little things. A kid's face will light up when you tell him that he did an excellent job on a quiz, especially when he has really been struggling with the subject matter. A little noticing goes a long way!

4 Really listen to your kids. Let kids know that you are paying attention to them and that what they have to say is important.

5 Help kids encourage themselves. Kids are often their own worst critics. Ask them if they are satisfied with their behavior and get them to give themselves some credit for things they are doing right.

TAKE A LOOK

at how many times you have acted as a lead-manager this week by encouraging your kids. This may be a tough one; it is much easier to criticize. Some of the ways I've encouraged my kid is by listening to her talk about how much homework she has, helping her find a costume for a school project, and attending her soccer game in the freezing cold. On the next page, add your own examples of how you have encouraged your kids this week. (If you can't think of anything you have done, think of things you will do.)

YOUR TURN

How have you encouraged your kids at home or at school this week?

Lead-managers recognize people when they are doing well. However, many people confuse RECOGNITION with PRAISE. We praise kids by flattering them because we want them to do something. This is a subtle form of coercion.* Kids resent flattery because they know there is an ulterior motive. If we want to help kids, we have to give up this kind of praise. On the other hand, recognition should be given to kids when they use...

EFFECTIVE

SUCCESSFUL

BEHAVIORS

*See *Restitution: Restructuring School Discipline* by Diane Gossen

We often do not recognize our kids when they act responsibly and independently because we overlook these behaviors ourselves. All of us have strong internal signals* that tell us when things are

RONG

For example, when a kid in your class hits another student, your pulse quickens, your face flushes, and you feel a surge of anger. These negative internal signals obviously indicate that there is a problem and that you need to deal with the student's behavior. However, we often ignore our internal signals when things are

RIGHT

Our brain still sends us positive internal signals when we see a kid acting responsibly, perhaps a sense of calm or a brief rush of pride, but these signals are usually much more subtle, and we don't pay attention to them. Therefore, as parents, teachers, and counselors, we need to stay in tune to the positive messages that our brains are sending us and help our kids identify what they are doing right!

*See *In Pursuit of Happiness* by E. Perry Good and *Control Theory: A New Explanation of How We Control Our Lives* by Dr. William Glasser.

SUCCESSFUL EFFECTIVE BEHAVIORS

- Acting responsibly
- Keeping commitments
- Being flexible
- Compromising
- Negotiating
- Making responsible decisions
- Setting goals
- Making plans
- Communicating effectively
- Caring about one's self and others

These are the behaviors that successful people use, yet they are often overlooked when our kids use them.

NOTHING SUCCEEDS LIKE SUCCESS

TAKE A LOOK

at your motives for the recognition you give your kids. Remember, there is a fine line between praise (a sneaky form of coercion) and recognition for effective, successful behaviors. For example, I saw a kid helping another student with a difficult math problem and I told her that she was being very helpful. I had no ulterior motive for the recognition I gave and the kid felt important because she was recognized. On the next page, give examples of how you have recognized your kids this week.

YOUR TURN

How have you paid attention to your positive internal signals and recognized kids for the things they have done right?

If our goal as parents, teachers, and counselors is to help kids become responsible and independent, the best help we can give them is to be lead-managers, both at home and at school. We can inform them about what they want to know, encourage them throughout the difficult process of growing up, and recognize them for their successful, effective behaviors.

The question then arises of how to help a kid who does not want to be managed, such as a student who has no interest in attending classes or a child who thinks that her parents are "really out of it." The answer is complicated and unique to each individual situation, but the key is to get involved and to stay involved with the kids we are trying to help.

CREATING INVOLVEMENT

CREATING INVOLVEMENT

It is impossible to help kids help themselves if you are not involved with them. What does it mean to be involved? Good Question!

WEBSTER DEFINES

INVOLVE

AS

TO MAKE INTRICATE OR COMPLICATED

TO AFFECT OR INCLUDE

Both of these definitions can apply to a relationship. In fact, a relationship which is not "intricate" and somewhat "complicated" is probably one in which both parties are not very involved.

Commonly, when thinking of relationships with our kids we think of the second definition of involve (to affect or include) and forget about the first (to make intricate or complicated). An involvement is difficult (the definition of "complicated") because both people have unique pictures of how they want the relationship to be. Many times, especially in relationships between adults and kids, these pictures are very different and constantly changing. The relationship a ten-year-old wants with his parents is different from the one he wants when he is fourteen. Parents tend to get stuck with the picture of the relationship with their ten-year-old and assume that is the way the picture will always be.

The key to any good solid relationship is admitting that it will CHANGE.

THE ONLY THING CONSTANT IN LIFE IS CHANGE.

There is no relationship that changes more than a parent-child relationship. Children are constantly growing mentally and physically, and parents must continuously adjust to these changes. When kids are little, the mental changes that are taking place are primarily learning about the tangible things in their worlds.

"Johnny, what does a cow say?"

"Moooooooooo!"

Parents delight in these changes; they clap when they hear "moo"! However, when kids reach the teenage years and start questioning their parents' values, the clapping stops and the arguing begins.

As kids become more aware of the world outside their family, they begin to realize they have choices, and what they value may not be what their parents value. Many times these changes are only temporary, but most parents get scared and make a big deal. Over the past twenty years I have been working with parents, teachers, and counselors of difficult teenagers. Some of these kids are juvenile delinquents and some of them are just plain difficult.

One question I ask myself is whether or not they get stuck acting like they value something they don't really believe in because adults make such a fuss. They essentially can't give up the act without losing face. They get stuck just trying out a new idea.

CHANGE

IS HARD FOR MANY ADULTS TO ACCEPT.

As a parent, the adoring child you were close to yesterday is now a teenager who hardly acknowledges your existence today. According to her, your duty is to provide food, shelter, clothes—and of course to leave her alone!

As a teacher or counselor who has established a good relationship with a kid, you may suddenly find that this connection doesn't seem to exist any longer. Kids rapidly change, trying to figure out what they really want and what is important to them. Adults have more or less figured out what they want and tend to forget that it isn't an easy task.

BEFORE

Constant and rapid change is particularly true of teenagers. Around the age of eleven or twelve, just when children are most compatible with the adults in their lives (when the adults' and the kids' pictures of the relationship match), the hormones begin raging, and what used to be important is no longer, such as doing ANYTHING with your parents.

AFTER

"I don't even know what people mean by adolescent. It seems to me, people nowadays jump from being a child to being an adult. You may not know that is what's happening, but it is. It's like going on an airplane. You can't tell anything is happening. You certainly don't know how fast you are going. You just sit there. Then they open the door and you're not where you are supposed to be. It doesn't seem like time is even moving, but you're not where you started out. That doesn't mean I feel like an adult. I don't know what that feels like. I just mean that I'm not where I was."

High School Student

Both our physical and psychological needs determine what is important to us. Our physical needs, such as food and shelter, help us to survive. Our psychological needs of love, power, fun, and freedom are vital to our mental health. We all have pictures of how we want to meet these needs.* Let's take a look at these basic mental needs and how to best think about them in RELATION to KIDS.

THINK of love and belonging as CONNECTION. This is the need to be connected to people, to be loved by a family member, to belong to a group, to be connected to a school—in general, TO BE A PART OF SOMETHING. Let's face it, we are not going to "love" anybody, even our own children, one hundred percent of the time. In fact, too much "love" can be suffocating, but we can ALWAYS keep a connection.

*See *In Pursuit of Happiness* by E. Perry Good and *Control Theory: A New Explanation of How We Control Our Lives* by Dr. William Glasser.

THINK of power as IMPORTANCE. Kids need to feel important both at school and at home. Normally the kids who are doing well grade-wise feel important in class, but they are not the majority of the student body. It is essential for every kid to have a sense of importance or competence. If we can't meet our psychological needs in long-term ways, we meet them short term through ineffective behaviors. For example, a kid may try to meet his need for importance by fighting at school. At home, parents often do not include kids in decisions, because "they are only children," thereby diminishing the kids' sense of importance in the family. Parents can help meet this need when kids' input is given consideration on questions as simple as what to have for dinner or as complicated as whether to move into a new house.

THINK...

of fun as PLAY. When kids are playing, adults often say, "STOP! You're making too much noise." Try to think of this play time as a means for kids to meet their needs. Yes, it can be loud, but is it hurting anyone? Our classrooms could safely be a bit noisier than they are. Unfortunately, the Puritans left us with the idea that if you are having fun, you aren't learning, working, or doing something meaningful. Actually, the reverse is true. These activities can and should be fun (at least part of the time). In fact, if you are not meeting ALL of your needs, you will most likely work LESS.

"You are troubled at seeing him spend his early years in doing nothing. What! Is it nothing to be happy? Is it nothing to skip, to play, to run about all day long? Never in all his life will he be so busy as now."

Jean Jacques Rousseau

THINK of freedom as INDEPENDENCE. One of the hardest concepts for parents, teachers, and counselors to grasp is that kids really NEED freedom, young children as well as teenagers. In order to grow up to be responsible adults, they need to be able to make their own choices and even their own mistakes.

"A bird in the cage soon forgets how to sing.

If you love me, give me wings."

Gary Morris

As adults who want to help and stay involved with kids, one of our main jobs is to create need-fulfilling environments. This means helping kids understand and meet all four of their basic psychological needs in a balanced way through effective behaviors. Adults can make kids aware that they have these needs, ask them to analyze how they are getting these needs met, and provide opportunities for them to get a sense of connection, importance, and independence and to have some fun.

TAKE A LOOK

at how you are dealing with your kids at home or at school. Think about the environment you are creating and how it is meeting the needs of kids. For example, when I do a workshop with kids, I always let them do an activity in which they talk to each other in small groups and share their ideas, opinions, and values. They feel connected and important, they are having fun, and they are doing the activity independently. On the next page, add some of the ways that you stay involved with kids by helping them meet their needs.

GO FOR IT

DO IT

JUMP

YOUR TURN

What are some of the ways you help create a need-fulfilling environment at home or at school?

PICTURES

If we want to stay involved, we have to be aware of our kid's pictures. When adolescence hits, it is as if a kid has a slide carousel in her head from which she has removed all the pictures that used to satisfy her needs. Everything from activities to parents and teachers to church attendance is up for re-examination.

CHANGING PICTURES

The kid begins to search for a new set of pictures that will meet her needs. Most of these new pictures contain friends rather than parents, teachers, or counselors. These are the pictures that establish the basis for independence and responsibility, even though many times this is hard for adults to believe. None of us has ever formed our own identity by staying dependent on the adults around us. The problem is that this is much harder to accept when YOU are the adult whose picture is being replaced.

STAYING INVOLVED

One key to staying involved with kids through these difficult changes is to understand what is happening. Remember that when a young person is changing his pictures of how he wants to meet his needs, the slide carousel is on the table and he is deciding which of his old pictures to leave in and which to take out. The slide of his parents is definitely "on the table." At this critical moment, if the parents judge or preach or yell or scream, the kid may just say, "I don't need this." Before the parents know it, their picture is OUT!

Frequently, parents are removed from their kid's slide carousel in the early teen years and don't get put back in until the kid is a young adult in their twenties. In a recent seminar, I was discussing this concept and a young professional woman said, "That's exactly what I did. I never understood it until you said that, but my mother was always on my back when I was a kid and finally I just removed her from my world. Now our relationship isn't bad, but for ten years I barely spoke to her. I realize that I could have used her help, but because she nagged me about essentially unimportant things, I didn't talk to her about what was important to me."

TAKE A LOOK

at how the pictures of either your own kids or your students are changing. It's not easy to keep "on top" of these things. For example, a father recently told me about his fifteen-year-old son whose world used to revolve around swimming. The father was able to stay involved with his son by taking an active interest in the sport. His son then informed him that he was quitting the swim team in order to devote more time to practicing with his rock band. Now the father is looking for new (and somewhat noisier) ways to stay involved with his son. On the next page, add some examples of your kids' changing pictures.

GO FOR IT

JUMP

YOUR TURN

What are some examples of pictures that your kids have recently replaced in their "slide carousel"?

In order to remain included in your kids' pictures as a need-fulfilling person, you have to stay involved. Adults frequently say, "Of course, I'm involved." or, "I have these kids in my class every day; I have to be involved." Seeing people daily does not mean that you are involved with them.

INVOLVEMENT = TIME + MEANING

To be truly involved with people, we have to spend time with them and talk about things that they think are important.

TIME

As parents are becoming increasingly busy, they are not able to spend as much time at home as parents once did. In order to justify this, someone invented the concept of "quality time." That is, "I don't have much time to spend with you, so let's make it meaningful."

Frankly, involvement does not work this way. Kids want their parents around as a backdrop to their lives. If you are there, sooner or later they will talk about something important, but not on demand or when it is convenient to you. You have to put in the time it takes to get involved.

Similarly, teachers have a very limited amount of time to spend with their kids. It is hard to make this time meaningful if you've only got fifty minutes to teach thirty or more students the history of the French Revolution. Unfortunately, this is the reality in most schools today. However, you can let kids know that if they do want to talk, you are willing to take the time to listen.

MEANING

Every now and then, when you are spending time with kids, something "meaningful" or important will...

Often this does not happen, and you cannot plan on it, but seize the moment if it does.

One way to put meaning into the time that you spend with kids is to participate in specific activities. Although I am not a big fan of homework just for the sake of it, I have had some very involving moments with my daughter while helping her with different school projects. For example, a recent assignment on the fashions and lifestyles of women in Victorian times led us to an interesting discussion on promiscuity. I have a choice as a parent to view this as a way to be involved with her or as an interruption to my busy schedule. Teachers can also take advantage of such moments to discuss values with their students. (Caution: this does not mean to "impose" values.)

Another activity that our family does takes place at the dinner table. For years my family has been doing "the best and the worst." This activity consists of each family member saying the best thing and the worst thing that happened to them that day. My daughter has never loved this activity (I cannot tell a lie!), but it promotes conversations other than, "Take your elbows off the table." Sometimes there is actually a "meaningful" conversation, but not every night.

There are many books with structured involvement activities in them. My favorite is *Values Clarification* by Sidney B. Simon, Leland W. Howe, and Howard Kirschenbaum.

Being involved with another person is not simply knowing "facts" about them, such as where they were born or how old they are. Remember that the definition of *involve* is "to make intricate or complicated." This includes knowing what they value and want. To know these things, we have to be willing to listen and to share our own values and wants with others.

When we are truly involved with another person, we know them on all three levels. Whether you are a parent, a teacher, or a counselor,

MAKE IT YOUR AIM

to know the facts, values, and wants of your kids.

THE INVOLVEMENT CIRCLE

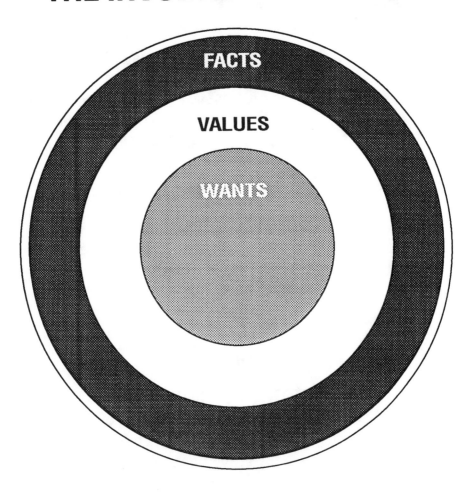

FACTS: occupation, hobbies, title of last book read, color of eyes, birthplace, family members

VALUES (or beliefs): politics, religion, art, sex, music

WANTS (or goals): to be happy, to be a good friend, to be a lawyer, to be responsible

TAKE A LOOK

at your relationship with the kids that you are involved with at home or at school. Do you know more facts about them than about what they value and want? Probably! I recently spoke with a counselor who was having difficulty with a student and I asked her if she knew the student on all three levels. She realized that she had plenty of information about the student's background, but didn't know what his beliefs and goals were. Think of a kid whom you are trying to help. On the next page, write down what you know about that kid on each level of involvement.

YOUR TURN

GO FOR IT

CHICKEN

YOUR TURN

What are some facts, values, and wants that a kid with whom you are involved has shared with you?

The most important link between becoming involved with kids and helping them help themselves is understanding the perceptual system, the quality world, and the inter-relationship between these two concepts. These strong influences on our lives are always with us, whether we know it or not, and our awareness of them is necessary if we want to give kids quality help. Therefore, in the next two chapters, we will be exploring perception and learning how to access the quality world.

EXPLORING PERCEPTION

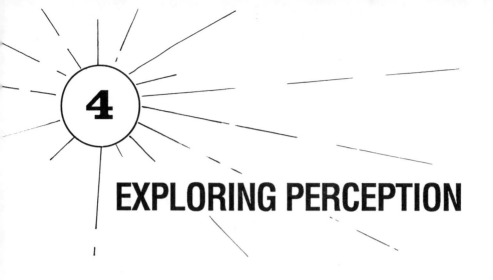

EXPLORING PERCEPTION

We see ourselves and the world around us with our perceptual system, though we are often unaware this system exists.

Right now, notice whether or not you are comfortable reading this book. Think about the chair in which you are sitting. Is it hard or soft? You have just brought your perceptual system into your awareness, but until I mentioned the chair (or is it the bed in which you are lying?) you were not aware of your sensory perceptions. If you are not too uncomfortable and you are interested in this book (I hope!), your lower levels of perception will go almost completely unnoticed.* In fact, we are unaware of our whole perceptual system most of the time.

WE TAKE IT FOR GRANTED

* See *Stations of the Mind: New Directions for Reality Therapy* by Dr. William Glasser

WHO'S CAUGHT WHO?

IT DEPENDS ON YOUR POINT OF VIEW

Our perceptual system is always there helping us make sense of the world, both

TANGIBLE AND INTANGIBLE

In the tangible world are things we can touch and in the intangible world are our concepts, ideas, and values. Most of us are fascinated with the stories about what happens when the perceptual system goes awry. Usually this is the result of some kind of brain injury, a stroke, or a tumor. Dr. Oliver Sacks has written popular books on this subject, *The Man Who Mistook His Wife for a Hat* and *Awakenings*. One reason that Dr. Sacks' books are so intriguing is that they cause us to think about something that is unthinkable—our brain gone haywire. This subject challenges all of our ideas about reality and who we are, because without a way to perceive ourselves, our lives have no meaning. In other words, if our perceptual system does not function, we do not function.

THE BIRD WHO MISTOOK HIS WIFE
FOR A HAT

Remember that our perceptual system is very subtle, but it is always there. If we are really in tune, we see that hints of perception show up in common phrases and everyday conversations all the time.

- "Do you see the glass as half empty or half full?"

- "Are you an optimist or a pessimist?"

- "How do you see it?"

- "What is your point of view?"

- "In my mind's eye..."

- "We don't see eye to eye."

- "That's not what I have in mind."

- "From my frame of reference..."

- "What is your interpretation?"

- "There has been a paradigm shift."

WHEN YOU HEAR THESE COMMENTS OR QUESTIONS, BE AWARE THAT THEY ARE AN ATTEMPT TO COMMUNICATE AND COMPARE OUR PERCEPTIONS.

LEVELS OF PERCEPTION

The perceptual system is a continuum of levels, ranging from the lowest to the highest.* All of our perceptions must first filter through the lowest, least complex levels before they can be perceived at the higher, more complicated levels. The lowest level of perception is the sensory system (touch, sight, sound, smell, and taste) and, as you move across the spectrum, the highest level is a system of values (beliefs and principles). At all levels of perception, we have pictures of how we would like to meet our needs. We store these pictures in a small part of the perceptual system called the QUALITY WORLD.

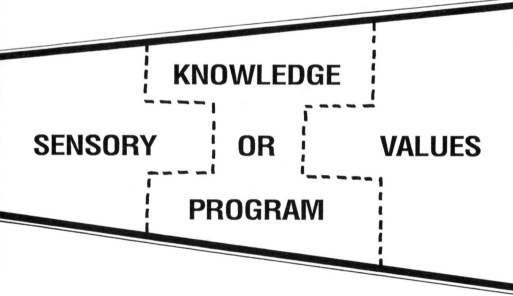

KNOWLEDGE

SENSORY   OR   VALUES

PROGRAM

*See *Behavior: The Control of Perception*
by William T. Powers

SENSORY LEVEL

At the sensory level, we have reference perceptions or pictures which tell us if the light is too dark or too bright, if a drink is too hot or too cold, and so on. Our perceptual system lets us know whether there is a match between what we want and what we are getting. We also have quality pictures of how we want to meet our needs at the sensory level. Take a moment to think about your favorite food. Even the word "favorite" lets you know that this is a picture in your quality world. Have you ever ordered this food at a restaurant, and when it was served, it wasn't at all what you had in mind? Old-time lemon meringue pie is one of my favorite foods in the whole world, but I never order it in restaurants because every time it is served, the filling looks like a congealed yellow brick and it tastes like sweetened lemon dishwashing detergent. It definitely does not meet the picture in my head of how a lemon meringue pie should look or taste. The only way to match my picture is for someone, preferably my mother, to make that pie from scratch.

LEMON
MERINGUE
PIE

KNOWLEDGE LEVEL

The mid level of perception is our knowledge filter. It is at this level that our brain holds information about sequential relationships, spatial relationships, and tangible objects. Our knowledge of sequential relationships tells us that in order to go to work, we first have to get in the car, put the key in the ignition, start the motor, and then pull out of the driveway. Our knowledge of the spatial relationships of tangible objects tells us that hats go on heads and shoes belong on our feet.

This type of information is "programmed" into our heads through our experiences. Everything we experience filters through our perceptual system and the perceptions that meet our needs become our quality world pictures. Pictures at this level include your favorite sweater, the route you drive to your best friend's house, and even the knowledge of how to brew coffee in the coffee maker.

WHAT YOU SEE...
...IS WHAT YOU GET

On these lower and mid levels of perception (sensory and knowledge), we have pictures that will meet our immediate needs, but not necessarily our long-term needs. For example, a teenager might have a quality picture of a sports car at the knowledge level. (Material possessions are at the mid levels of perception.) If she drops out of school to earn more money to buy the car, she will get her quality picture at one level of perception. However, she runs a big chance of feeling dissatisfied with herself later, when she does not have a high school degree and her reality does not match her concept of a successful person.

VALUES LEVEL

The highest level of perception is the values level, where we find our beliefs or what we "hold sacred." At this level are the quality pictures of specifically the kind of people we want to be, such as happy, successful, strong, or responsible. We also have specific pictures of how we want our relationships to be at the values level. For example, a woman might have a picture of the relationship with her husband where they are equally responsible for all decision making. This is a part of her concept of a successful marriage. At this level our pictures primarily have to do with how we see ourselves in relation to the rest of the world. Rather than material possessions, these are pictures of people and activities. The best way to meet our long-term needs is to look at our pictures on the values level.

TAKE A LOOK

at your quality world pictures at all levels of perception. For example, at the sensory level I have pictures of country music and the color purple. At the knowledge level I have pictures of my Dodge van and traveling to the beach. At the values level I have pictures of being a good mother and a successful speaker. On the next page, add some of your pictures at the different levels of perception.

YOUR TURN

What are your quality world pictures at the sensory, knowledge, and values levels of perception?

SENSORY

KNOWLEDGE

VALUES

WHAT DOES PERCEPTION
HAVE TO DO
WITH HELPING KIDS?

EVERYTHING

Until we understand the perceptual system and how it
influences the way we meet our needs, we can't help
kids help themselves.

Remember that all of us have the same basic psychological needs of love, power, fun, and freedom. These needs were developed in our earliest ancestors. Some anthropologists call them "social needs."

GENERALLY

The ways we meet our needs seem remarkably similar around the world. In almost all cultures and throughout history, these needs are met through traditions such as marriage, work, art, music, and food.

SPECIFICALLY

Our pictures are amazingly different. From Beethoven's fifth symphony to hard rock. From a painting by Renoir to pictures on a cave wall. From enchiladas to sushi. Depending on our culture and our individual tastes, we all have very unique and creative need-fulfilling pictures.

Think of our needs as undeveloped film. From the minute we are born, we are perceiving the world and taking pictures of people, things, and behaviors that will help us meet our needs. We store these pictures in our quality world "photo albums."

Then all of us, kids included, try to make our quality world pictures a reality. Because our pictures are unique, actualizing them is the cause of a lot of teacher-student and parent-child conflict. The perceptual system explains why an adult's picture of help can be so different from that of a kid.

For example, my picture of a quality relationship with my teenage daughter is one in which she confides in me, because then I can help her. I want to hear all about what's going on in her life. Yet, she chooses to share this information with her friends. Confiding in her mother is not one of her pictures, BUT confiding in her friends is a LARGE picture in her quality world (if the number of hours she spends on the telephone is any indication).

Teens: Talk, Tunes, and Tee Vee

CONWAY, S.C. —

According to a profile of 1,237 delegates to the National Association of Student Councils, student leaders spend an average 8.4 hours a day on entertainment and socializing. The survey taken at a conference of high school leaders reveals that they spend four hours a day listening to music and 2.4 hours watching TV.

The study also reveals that talking on the telephone consumes an average of two hours of a student's day—with girls talking a half-hour more than boys.

▼ continued on 3B

In order to have a quality relationship with my daughter, I have to find some pictures that are important to both of us, and build our relationship on those. We might play tennis or jog together. However, if I begin to nag her about not confiding in me, she may not want to do these activities with me. If I say, "Daughters SHOULD confide in their mothers," what I am really telling her is that my picture is right, and her picture is wrong.

"I may not be aware of how you see things—and of the importance of understanding how you see things. The less I know, the more likely I am to underestimate how little I know. Like a city I have never visited, the inside of someone else's mind is terra incognita. It is so unknown that I am unlikely to appreciate how unknown it is. Nor am I likely to appreciate how important it is to our relationship for me to explore that territory and learn what I can about it."

Roger Fisher and Scott Brown, *Getting Together*

117

The only pictures we can perceive are our own. Here's an odd example, but one that illustrates how subtle our perceptual systems are:

WHAT YOU ARE NOW READING IS

MY

PERCEPTION

OF

PERCEPTION

This statement sounds strange, but it is true of everything you read. What you read is the author's perception of a subject. Perception is a topic on which there are many different opinions; there is no absolute right or wrong. I have studied and read about perceptual systems for many years, but most of what I am writing comes from my own experiences with my clients, my family, my friends, and myself using the ideas which I have learned about this subject. Awareness of the levels of perception, in even the broadest sense, can help us understand ourselves and others as we never have before.

AWARENESS is a key word. Most of the time we are totally unaware of our perceptual system. The more we recognize that it is operating non-stop and that it is always influencing our pictures, the better chance we have of helping ourselves and our kids. Each of us is trying to get the "real" world to be the same as the perfect world (or quality world) in our heads. The pictures of our relationships with either our own kids or our students rarely match our "real" relationships. This is often because the kids with whom we are involved do not act as we would like. If our pictures focus on how others should behave, we may have difficulties because, ultimately, we can only control ourselves and our own perceptions.

For example, a mother came to see me for counseling because her son had a Mohawk haircut and a pierced ear. This was not her picture of how her son should look. I asked her if he was doing OK in school and if he was involved in any extracurricular activities. She said he was getting good grades and was active in sports. When I asked her how their relationship was, she said, "It was great until he cut his hair like THAT and pierced his ear. Now, all I do is nag him because every time I see him I want to burst into tears." Did she honestly think that he would have a Mohawk forever? No. Did she want to have a good relationship with her son forever? Yes. When confronted with the reality that he was not yet ready to give up his  Mohawk, she realized that she could either make the relationship worse by not giving up her "picture" of him and continuing to nag, or make it better by recognizing that the relationship with him was more important in the long run than how he currently looked.

*"You may give them your love, but not your thoughts,
For they have their own thoughts."*

Kahlil Gibran

Getting rid of the idea of "right" and "wrong" pictures
is a very difficult task. As parents, teachers, and coun-

selors, we have many opinions about right and wrong which we have formed through our own experiences. Frequently, I hear adults say, "But I know that is bad for her." Unfortunately, what is "bad for her" may be a short-term way for her to meet a need. For example, smoking pot with friends may be satisfying on the sensory level of perception and may meet the kid's need for belonging at that moment. However, smoking pot may interfere with some of her higher level pictures, such as being successful or responsible. Nevertheless, it is her picture and we cannot change it or remove it from her world. She must do that for herself.

Think about when you were a teenager. Do you remember what was important to you then? Those were your quality world pictures. Do you remember how important it was to feel included?

I was very fat as a teenager and didn't have a boyfriend until I was sixteen. Finally I got one! I think it was because I helped him with his math homework. Nevertheless, he was mine! I walked him off the football field, and he kissed me. It was heaven, because...

I WAS JUST LIKE EVERYBODY ELSE

As I became older, I wasn't very interested in conforming. I wanted to be different.

YOU DON'T HAVE THE SAME PERCEPTIONS NOW THAT YOU HAD WHEN YOU WERE A KID, AND YOUR KID'S PERCEPTIONS WON'T STAY THE SAME EITHER

(Don't forget this information; it can get you through some hard times.)

Many times when adults are trying to help kids, they don't communicate their own picture. Instead, they communicate what is "wrong." In your head, you have a perception of how you want things to be, just as your kids have their own perceptions. For example, you want your kid to wear a presentable outfit to her grandmother's house. However, your picture of a presentable outfit is very different from that of your kid. Instead of telling her your picture, you wait until she is dressed and then say...

TAKE A LOOK

at how often you share your pictures with your kids at home or at school. For example, a teacher tells his students that there will be a substitute teacher instructing the class. He communicates what he expects them to accomplish and discusses his picture of appropriate behavior. By informing the students beforehand, the teacher has a much better chance of returning to find a positive report from a grateful substitute teacher rather than having to discipline his students. On the next page, add your own pictures that you have communicated to your kids.

JUMP

IT'S EASY

YOUR TURN

What are some of your pictures that you have shared with your kids?

"Somewhere along the line of development, we discover what we really are, and then we make our real decision for which we are responsible. Make that decision primarily for yourself because you can never really live anyone else's life, not even your own child's. The influence you exert is through your own life and what you become yourself."

Eleanor Roosevelt

126

Kids, as well as the rest of us, have quality world pictures at all levels of perception. These pictures have many different names: reference perceptions, wants, ideas, concepts, goals, beliefs, etc. If we focus only on the lower and mid levels of perception, we will get what we want for the moment and will probably be happy for a while. But this type of success can be fleeting. It is at the values level that we find pictures of long-term happiness, strength, success, and responsibility. The next chapter focuses on helping kids access their quality world pictures at all levels, but most importantly at the values level.

ACCESSING THE QUALITY WORLD

5

ACCESSING THE QUALITY WORLD

Our most powerful ally when helping ourselves and others is the highest level of perception. The values level houses that elusive, but all-important, factor in life. . .

MOTIVATION

MOTIVATION

MOTIVATION

There are few topics related to kids that get as much attention as this one. How many times have you heard, "I just can't motivate the kids in my class; they don't want to learn anything I am trying to teach them," or "I don't know what to do with my daughter; I can't even motivate her to clean up her room."?

As adults, we often believe that it is our job to motivate kids. However, this is an impossible task and it is not within our power. Although most of us intuitively *know* this, we keep TRYING to "motivate" kids externally. It is a difficult notion to give up.

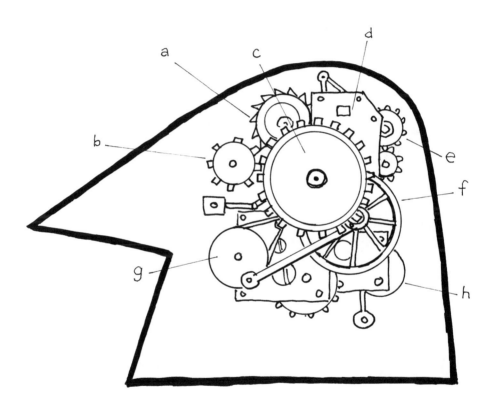

We have to remember that all of us are INTERNALLY motivated. If we understand that motivation comes from our quality world and understand how this works, then we have a good chance of using this information to help kids help themselves.

THE MOST POWERFUL MOTIVATION comes from what we value. It is intangible and it is related to our basic psychological needs of belonging, power, fun, and freedom. These needs developed in our earliest ancestors as they cooperated and competed with each other. Meeting these needs was social in nature, not material. (There were no Cadillacs in the caves.) From these social needs came our pictures of how we want to see ourselves and how we want others to see us. These basic psychological needs drive our internal system.* We delude ourselves if we believe that we can motivate kids from the outside. Yet, we attempt to motivate them with all sorts of rewards, from candy bars to cars.

*See *Control Theory: A New Explanation of How We Control Our Lives* by Dr. William Glasser.

We continue deluding ourselves because sometimes these "carrots" work, but only for a short while. Kids resent being bribed, and adults resent feeling like they HAVE to bribe kids. Hooking into a kid's internal motivation isn't easy. In fact, it is probably the biggest challenge we have when living and working with kids.

Just as we cannot help kids by giving them external rewards, we also cannot motivate them by using coercive behaviors, such as flattery. These behaviors are an attempt to control our kids and are therefore countereffective.

To help kids motivate themselves, we have to learn how to access the quality world at the values level. A large part of what we call "help" does not connect to our kid's quality world at the highest level of perception. Often "help" takes the form of giving advice or telling the kid what (or what not) to do. The kid sits there, nodding his head, saying, "I won't do it again," or "I'll try to do better. Can I leave now?" The adult assumes that the kid who is receiving the advice wants to BE just like the kid in the adult's quality world picture. Most kids have little or no intention of being that "perfect" kid. They may pretend to agree with the adult's advice because they have learned that it is easier than arguing and provides the path of least resistance. Even if they do try to follow the advice of adults, they are not matching their own pictures. Kids may do better for a while following someone else's idea of how they should be. Then, to use a great old Southern expression, they

BACKSLIDE

TAKE A LOOK

at the times when you have attempted to motivate your kids at home or at school. What techniques do you tend to use most? Flattery, presents (bribery), threats? Most adults have built up quite a repertoire of external motivators. Do these tactics work? The grocery store is a wonderful place to observe a wide variety of "motivational" techniques being used by exasperated parents. These include parents spanking their children and shoving bags of candy in the kids' hands. On the next page, add your own examples of ways in which you try to motivate your kids.

GO FOR IT

YOUR TURN

HMMM

YOUR TURN

What external motivators do you use? Identify your personal "favorite" and add two more that you use when your first choice doesn't work.

FIRST I...

THEN I...

THEN, IN TOTAL DESPERATION, I...

Our strongest motivation is linked to our desire for personal happiness and success which comes from the values level. Therefore, we need to understand our perceptual system at this level—no easy task!

In the last chapter you took a moment to think about the chair in which you were sitting. This brought the sensory level of perception into your awareness. Now ask yourself the question, "Do I want to be happy?" You may answer this question with an immediate "Yes!" or you may first think about what your picture of happy is and then say, "Of course I want to be happy." This question has brought your highest level of perception into your awareness. We take for granted that we want to be happy, but do not think about the fact that this desire comes from our quality world pictures at the values level.

Think of the highest level of perception as being divided into two tiers: values and a system of values. (Remember that the levels of the perceptual system build upon each other.) Our values are our guiding principles and fundamental beliefs. Our system of values is the sum total of our principle and beliefs.

SYSTEM OF VALUES

This part of our perceptual system is the most difficult to understand and access. The pictures here are not only intangible, but they may also be instinctual.* At the system of values level, most people share some general fundamental ideas of how we envision our "ideal" selves and our "perfect" relationships. These concepts have probably been built into humans over the ages.

*See *Behavior: The Control of Perception*
by William T. Powers.

The system of values is where we find our VISION of what we want to BE and the overall direction of where we want our lives to go.

"And what is good, and what is not good—need we ask anyone to tell us these things?"   Robert Pirsig

Everyone wants to BE happy, successful, strong, responsible, and to have good relationships. If you question this statement, think about whether you know anyone who *honestly* wants to be miserable, unhappy, weak, irresponsible, or to have a horrible relationship. In other words, we all want quality lives. We may not know how to go about living quality lives, we may not even think that it is possible. Nevertheless, it is what we want. We know that kids also want to be happy, yet we rarely ask them to describe the overall direction they want to take their lives.

In his book *Zen and the Art of Motorcycle Maintenance: An Inquiry into Values*, Robert Pirsig maintains that "even though quality cannot be defined, you know what quality is!" Though kids have a sense of what quality is, they may not be willing to admit that it is something that they value or that they want in their lives. This is territory that adults rarely explore with kids.

Stephen Covey describes quality as a fundamental principle in his book *The Seven Habits of Highly Effective People*. Covey believes that there are principles such as fairness, honesty, and integrity that cut across all cultures. We are all born with this territory within our perceptual system.

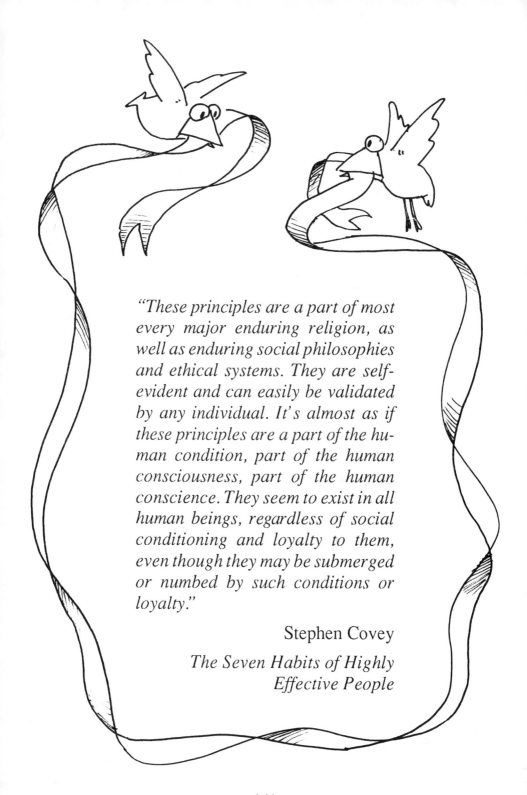

"These principles are a part of most every major enduring religion, as well as enduring social philosophies and ethical systems. They are self-evident and can easily be validated by any individual. It's almost as if these principles are a part of the human condition, part of the human consciousness, part of the human conscience. They seem to exist in all human beings, regardless of social conditioning and loyalty to them, even though they may be submerged or numbed by such conditions or loyalty."

Stephen Covey

The Seven Habits of Highly Effective People

When adults do discuss such things as quality, values, or principles with kids, it is usually in terms of the adults' pictures of these concepts, not in terms of the kids' pictures. These discussions can easily turn into a lecture or a sermon rather than an open-ended, two-way conversation.

Many of the delinquent teenagers that I have worked with over the last twenty years have never explored this territory within themselves. They look at the world in a superficial way, not at the values level of perception. For example, a kid might say he wants to be a drug dealer so he can drive a big car and make a lot of money. This may sound like his vision of what he wants to be, but don't be fooled. This is not a picture of the overall direction he wants his life to go. The car and the money are pictures at the knowledge level and will never provide the kid with long-term success. His pictures at the values level are NOT what is motivating him to sell drugs.

As parents, teachers, and counselors, it is our job to bring the quality world into our kids' awareness and keep them conscious of their overall direction. Are the choices they make leading them toward failure or toward success, happiness, and responsibility? Even young children can understand the concept of overall direction, but WE have to make them aware of it.

HOW DO YOU HELP KIDS ACCESS THEIR QUALITY WORLD?

The word *access* means "the right to enter or use." We cannot either "enter" or "use" another person's quality world, but we can access our own and help our kids learn how to access theirs.

The first principle in exploration is a belief that the territory is there to be discovered, that kids do have a concept of the overall direction in which they want their lives to go.

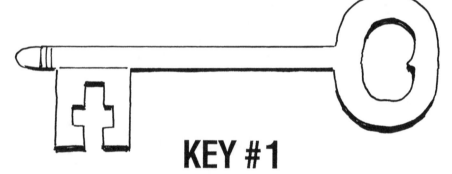

KEY #1

EXPLORE THE TERRITORY

If Columbus had not believed that there was some territory out there to be discovered, he would not have set off from Spain in three small boats across the Atlantic. As helping adults, at times we may have little faith that the territory is there, that the values quality world really exists in the head of THIS kid. Don't give up, it's really there!

A consultant at an alternative school that only handles very tough kids provides an example. Tina, a fifteen-year-old prostitute, was a student in this school. She was very beautiful, looked older than she was, and lived in a town with many visiting businessmen who had money and time to spend. She had been arrested and was "serving time" in this institution. The young counselor who was working with her tried repeatedly to get her to "admit" that she did not really want to be a prostitute in her "heart of hearts" (another name for her values quality world). Tina stuck to her guns; she said that she enjoyed being a prostitute, and, furthermore, she

had earned almost $30,000 last year. She then asked the counselor (an attractive twenty-five-year-old woman) how much money she made last year. When Tina heard the $15,000 figure, she suggested that perhaps the counselor might want to join her in her line of work; it was certainly more lucrative than counseling!

In exasperation, the counselor asked the consultant what she should do. The consultant's advice hinged on the belief that Tina had a values quality world, even though Tina was essentially denying it's existence. The counselor needed to access this world if she wanted to help her. This is the conversation that took place between Tina and her counselor:

> Counselor: "Do you want to get married when you are older?"
>
> Tina: "Yes."
>
> Counselor: "And when you are married, do you want to have children?"
>
> Tina: "Yes."
>
> Counselor: "And when you have a child—let's say that it's a girl—it's fine with you if your daughter becomes a prostitute when she's fifteen, right?"
>
> Tina (screaming): "Don't talk about my daughter like that!"

Tina then burst into tears and said that she was miserable being a prostitute, but did not know what else to do to earn money. She went on to say, "I don't want to be like this; I want to be happy like other people. I feel bad about myself." This kind of awareness comes from Tina exploring the overall direction in which she wants to take her life.

Clearly some of our pictures on the lower levels of perception are in conflict with our pictures on the higher levels. Sometimes this conflict is very painful. We do not think we can get our pictures at the values level so we try to satisfy our needs only through pictures at the lower levels of perception. We don't think about the overall direction we are taking our lives and focus only on the immediate benefits. In Tina's case, prostitution enabled her to buy possessions that were in her quality world, but they did not satisfy her needs in the long term. However, she knew that she wanted to be proud of herself in her...

HEART OF HEARTS

Once Tina brought her system of values into her awareness, she was on her way to figuring out what she could do to move her life in the overall direction of long-term happiness and success that would meet her needs at the values level of perception. Searching for this territory can be quite an adventure, and many times kids need an adult to guide them to (or at least point them in the direction of) this unexplored terrain.

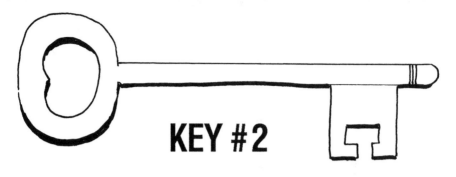

KEY #2

GREAT EXPECTATIONS

Sometimes there is an unwillingness on the part of helping adults to try to access the REAL quality world of kids. They wonder if they are pushing the kids too hard or if they are opening up possibilities that the kids may be unable to reach. Some of us work with young people whose futures SEEM very limited. But if we understand the origin of motivation, we know that the most limiting barriers to success are internal. People do succeed in spite of great social, economic, racial, gender, and physical odds. These people do not limit themselves to someone else's low expectations. In fact, they have probably been helped by a parent, a teacher, or a counselor who truly believed in them.

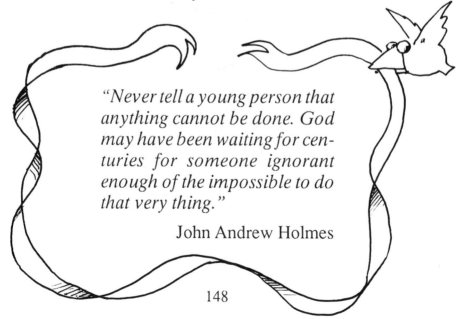

"Never tell a young person that anything cannot be done. God may have been waiting for centuries for someone ignorant enough of the impossible to do that very thing."

John Andrew Holmes

Let's take a look at the word

EXPECTATIONS

This term can have good or bad connotations, depending on the way it is used. Expectations can be used as an external motivator by attempting to cause anxiety or to make a kid feel guilty. "I expect you to do very well on your next test. If you don't, you'll fail this course," or "I had such high expectations for you. I'm so disappointed that you aren't going to medical school." These comments are coercive, trying to get a kid to be what YOU want her to be, and do not help the kid access her own quality world.

On the other hand, expecting the best from a kid by believing in her ability can be a great help in accessing a kid's quality world. Having high expectations may be just what is needed by a kid who is limiting herself by her own low expectations.

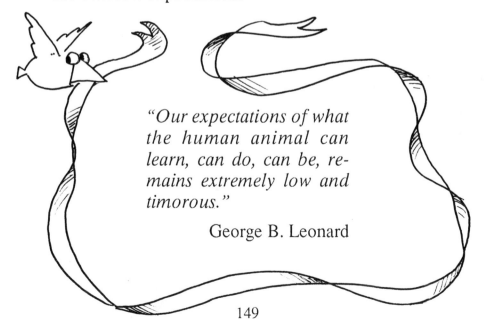

"Our expectations of what the human animal can learn, can do, can be, remains extremely low and timorous."

George B. Leonard

TAKE A LOOK

at what you expect from your kids at home or at school. How do you express your expectations? Is it in terms of your picture of what you want your kid to be? ("I expected that you would call if you were going to be late. Why can't you be more responsible?") Or is it in terms of your belief in their quality world pictures? ("I know that you want to learn to play guitar; I think you'll do great!") On the next page, give examples of what you expect from your kids and whether these expectations come from your pictures or theirs.

YOUR TURN

What are some expectations you've discussed with your kids? Did these discussions help your kids access their quality world?

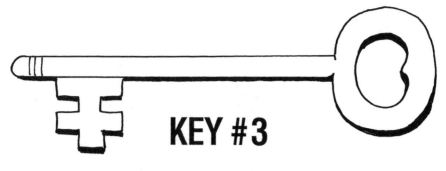

KEY #3

DEVELOP PICTURES

How can you say that you want to be successful if you have not thought about how your picture of success would look? As helping adults, it is crucial that we discuss with our kids the overall direction in which they would like to go. These discussions help them develop their pictures of personal and inter-personal success.

Often parents say that their children have no idea of what they want to be. Yet most parents do not discuss careers possibilities with their kids. Very young children often get asked, "What do you want to be when you grow up?" For some reason, as the child grows older, we stop asking this question. However, this is exactly when we should seriously begin discussing this topic!

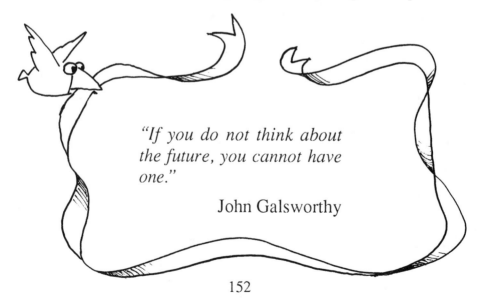

"If you do not think about the future, you cannot have one."

John Galsworthy

Discussing a kid's future goes beyond exploring careers. We can also help kids develop pictures of the kind of relationships they want to have and the kind of people they want to be in these relationships (caring, loving, supportive). Kids can certainly use our help when developing their vision of themselves and their quality world.

TAKE A LOOK

at how you can help your kids develop their pictures at the values level. For example, a teacher can introduce quality to his students by first discussing what quality schoolwork is. Once students begin to think about their concept of quality, they can then move to broader questions. What is a quality relationship? What is a quality life? On the next page, add your own ideas of how you can help kids develop their pictures, and then make a plan to implement these ideas.

TAKE OFF

JUST JUMP

CLOSE YOUR EYES

IT WON'T HURT

YOUR TURN

What are some possible opportunities for you to help your kids develop their pictures at the values level?

Understanding the perceptual system and the quality world is a continual process of learning, growing, and looking inward. These concepts provide the backdrop for self-evaluation. When we understand that we are internally motivated, we can see that evaluating ourselves is the most important and powerful form of analysis. Therefore, helping kids includes teaching them the valuable skill of self-evaluation.

LEARNING
SELF-EVALUATION

157

LEARNING SELF-EVALUATION

Self-evaluation is an idea whose time has not yet come. A fundamental problem with the way many adults try to help kids is that the adults are evaluating the behavior of the kids, instead of having the kids evaluate themselves.

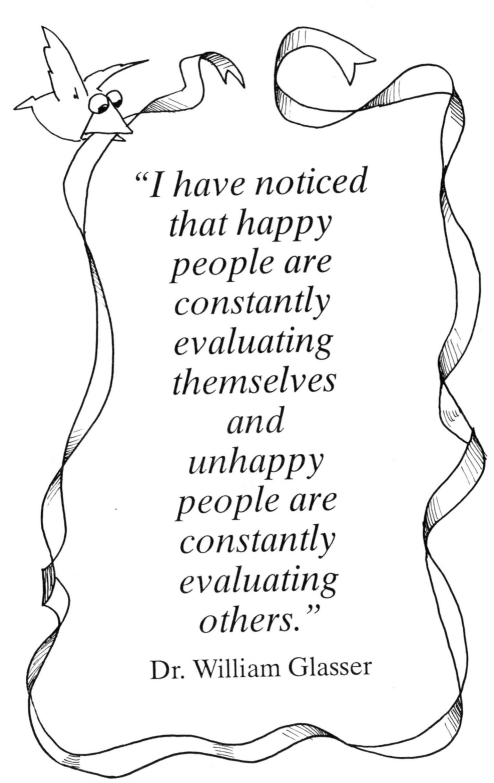

"I have noticed that happy people are constantly evaluating themselves and unhappy people are constantly evaluating others."

Dr. William Glasser

Self-evaluation is the most effective way to motivate a change in behavior because the analysis comes from within the kid's head, rather than from an external source.

But society places a great amount of emphasis on external assessments. Bosses monitor their employees' progress. Teachers test and assess their students. Parents judge their children's behavior. We continue evaluating others with a great amount of fervor, believing that this is the way to help, to initiate change.

Think about yourself and the people you know in reference to Dr. Glasser's statement on the previous page. Think about the happy people you know. They are continually looking for ways to improve themselves. On the other hand, unhappy people seem to always be looking outside themselves at what is wrong, primarily blaming those around them.

THE BIG QUESTION IS

What kind of kids do you want to be raising, teaching, or counseling? The kind who evaluate other people or the kind who evaluate themselves? Do we want kids who are constantly blaming everyone else for their problems or kids who are able to analyze their problems and find solutions?

THE BIG ANSWER IS

Of course we want happy kids who are skilled at self-evaluation. We also want to help our kids become happy, responsible, and independent adults. (Then, hopefully, they won't move back in with us!)

How do we teach kids self-evaluation, especially if we don't have much practice at evaluating ourselves?

Perhaps that's the answer. Learn how to evaluate yourself. Once you make self-evaluation a positive habit in your own life, it will be much easier to teach this skill to kids. What they see you doing now is evaluating others, primarily them! However, if they see you practicing and modeling self-evaluation . . .

...this skill just might RUB OFF on the kids.

If you are a teacher, you may be thinking, "But it is my job to evaluate students and to grade their work." This is true of the way things currently stand in most schools, but why shouldn't kids participate in the evaluation of their own work? Some of us may be uncomfortable with this idea, but it is the only way we will ever arrive at quality work in our schools.*

If you are a parent, you may be thinking, "But how will my children learn what is right if they do not know what they have done wrong? It is my parental duty to evaluate them." Children will learn far more from your example than from your criticism. Rely less on your analysis of their behavior, and start asking them questions that will lead to their own self-analysis. When they take an honest look at themselves, they are more likely to change their behavior, which is, after all, why you evaluate them in the first place.

"Children have never been very good at listening to their elders. But they have never failed to imitate them."

James Baldwin

*See *The Quality School: Managing Students Without Coercion* by Dr. William Glasser.

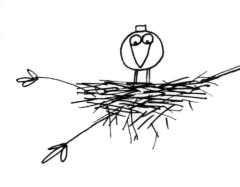

TAKE A LOOK

at how often you evaluate kids. An important step towards reducing your reliance on evaluating others is REALIZING when you are doing it. One night at 9:30 p.m. my daughter informed me that she had to take a semester exam in Algebra the next day for which she had not begun to study. I immediately evaluated her behavior by saying, "Why didn't you study on Saturday, instead of watching the basketball tournament? I'm sure you knew you had a test tomorrow." Think of situations where you chose to evaluate kids' behaviors, instead of encouraging them to analyze their own actions.

YOUR TURN

JUST JUMP

YOUR TURN

What are some times that you have evaluated the behavior of your kids at home or at school? (Your kids can probably help you out with this one.)

1

To evaluate or not to evaluate ....

2

....that is the question.

3

What is the point of evaluating yourself?

4

...'tis the only way to a quality life.

5

Why?

6

Remember the per-
ceptual system and
the quality world?

7

Only you can evaluate
yourself in relation
to your perceptions
and pictures.

8

Alas, no one else can
do this for you.

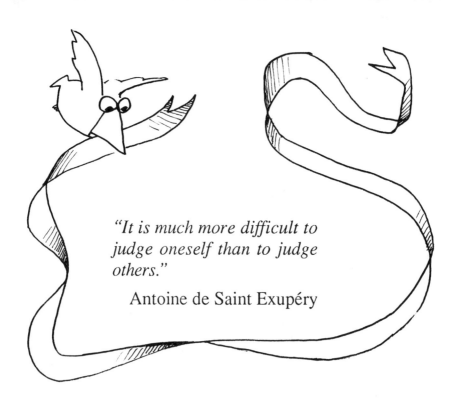

"It is much more difficult to judge oneself than to judge others."

Antoine de Saint Exupéry

SELF-EVALUATION

is a matter of asking yourself questions and answering them honestly. This includes focusing on your perceptions at the values level. You can then help kids go through the same process.

The Reality Therapy model, developed by Dr. William Glasser, asks questions which lead people to analyze their own behavior.* This model can easily be applied by parents, teachers, and counselors. The best way to help kids is to steer them towards self-assessment, which is the path to becoming a responsible, effective person.

*See *Reality Therapy* by Dr. William Glasser.

AN OVERVIEW OF QUESTIONS TO ASK YOURSELF

What do I want?

What am I doing to get what I want?

Is my behavior getting me what I want?

At first these questions may seem deceptively simple, but they are at the heart of any self-evaluation process. No matter what the endeavor, if you don't know what you want, then you won't get it. Even if you do know what you want, but you are using ineffective behaviors, then you still won't get it. This is true for quality work as well as a quality relationship or a quality life. Sounds easy, right? Wrong! The answers to these questions can be quite complicated.

Let's look at these questions in more detail by applying them to your own life and by looking at how kids might answer them.

WHAT DO I WANT?

I have found that this question has more flexibility if it is divided into *overall direction* and *specific wants* for two reasons. First, this may make it easier for you to answer this sometimes difficult question. Second, this question can then be tied directly to the QUALITY WORLD PICTURES at the values level of perception, which is where meaningful self-evaluation must start.

Part I: OVERALL DIRECTION

What do I want to be overall? What is the overall direction in which I want to move my life?

Possible answers are:

"I want to move in the direction of happiness, success, strength, responsibility, doing my best, or being in a quality relationship." It is imperative that we ask ourselves this question because it forms the basis of self-evaluation. If you don't keep the overall goal in mind then the answer is often superficial and is not based on the higher levels of perception.

172

For example, frequently kids say their school work is "good enough." Good enough for whom? The teacher, of course. When a student's work is only rated through test scores and teachers' assessments, these evaluations have little meaning to the kid. If he is judged to be a "poor" or "average" student, he does enough work to "get by." If he is considered to be a "good" student, he does enough work to maintain his status in the class. In our present system, students see little incentive to excel above and beyond what is "expected" of them. The students are not encouraged to focus on their own quality world pictures. In this case, the question to ask is, "Do I want to be moving in the direction of doing my best and being successful?" If so, then is "good enough" what I want?

"We only lose our way when we lose our aim."

Francois Fenelon

What do I want?

Part II: SPECIFIC WANTS

What do I want specifically? If I were successful or doing my best, what would it look like?

Although we are often not aware of it, we all have very specific pictures of how we want our lives to be. Remember the concept of the territory? That is where we find these pictures, but first we have to develop, explore, and access them.

When we begin by focusing on the overall direction, it is much easier to then get the specific picture. When kids are asked what they want, the answer is often, "Nothing," or "I don't know." But when asked, "Do you want to be happy?" the answer is always, "Yes." They may go on to say, "But I don't know HOW."

Then ask these questions:

• What would it be like if you were happy?

• What exactly would be going on in your life?

The specific picture can be difficult to put into focus. Sometimes it is painful to admit, even to ourselves, what we want that we don't have. This is why involvement is so essential when working with kids. If you have an open, honest relationship with a kid, he will be much more receptive to your assistance in exploring his quality world pictures.

What am I doing to get what I want?

To answer this question, you must "name the behavior."
We often use ineffective behaviors without even realizing that we have chosen them. In fact, most of us do not even think of them as...

WE THINK OF THEM AS...

such as depressed, anxious, worried, mad, insulted, or sick. A "condition" is something that just happens to us, something we have no control over. A "behavior" is something that we choose to do (or choose not to do). If we learn to identify these behaviors, we can then evaluate whether they are helping us get what we want. In the long run, being depressed, mad, anxious, or worried rarely gets us the results for which we are looking.*

*See *Control Theory: A New Explanation of How We Control Our Lives* by Dr. William Glasser and *In Pursuit of Happiness* by E. Perry Good for a more detailed description of the behavioral system.

Let's see how these questions work by starting with a simple example. I want to be a good tennis player. This would make me happy because then I could play tennis with my husband. My specific picture of being a good tennis player is being able to serve the ball and volley the ball eight to ten times. What am I doing right now to get what I want? I am thinking about being a better tennis player. I am sitting in my house wishing that I could play a better game of tennis, and I am slightly depressed that I can't play better than I do. This leads us to the final self-evaluation question.

Is my behavior getting me what I want?

This question is the core of self-evaluation, but without the previous questions, it is not effective. It asks you to take a closer look at what you are doing and to relate your current behavior to getting what you want.

If I continue sitting, wishing, and being depressed, do I have a chance of becoming a better tennis player? Will these behaviors get me what I want? It is highly doubtful.

WHAT WILL HELP ME GET WHAT I WANT? Which behaviors can I use to improve my tennis game? This begins my quest for more effective behaviors which will allow me to reach my goal and fulfill my need for power or competence. I can practice with a friend who plays tennis at about my level of ability. I can take lessons. I can hit balls against a backboard.

GET THE IDEA?

When you face the reality that your current behaviors are ineffective, you can then brainstorm for new behaviors, make a plan, and actively pursue what you want.

TAKE A LOOK

at how you can begin practicing self-evaluation so that you can then teach your kids this skill. Think about something you want. Then ask yourself the questions on page 171 to see if your behavior is effective. Start with something small (such as planting a garden or improving a skill). Then you can move on to the "big stuff" when you have some practice under your belt (such as doing your best at your job or having a successful marriage).

YOUR TURN

GO FOR IT

TAKE OFF

JUMP

YOUR TURN

WHAT DO I WANT OVERALL?

WHAT DO I WANT SPECIFICALLY?

WHAT AM I DOING TO GET WHAT I WANT?

IS MY BEHAVIOR GETTING ME WHAT I WANT?

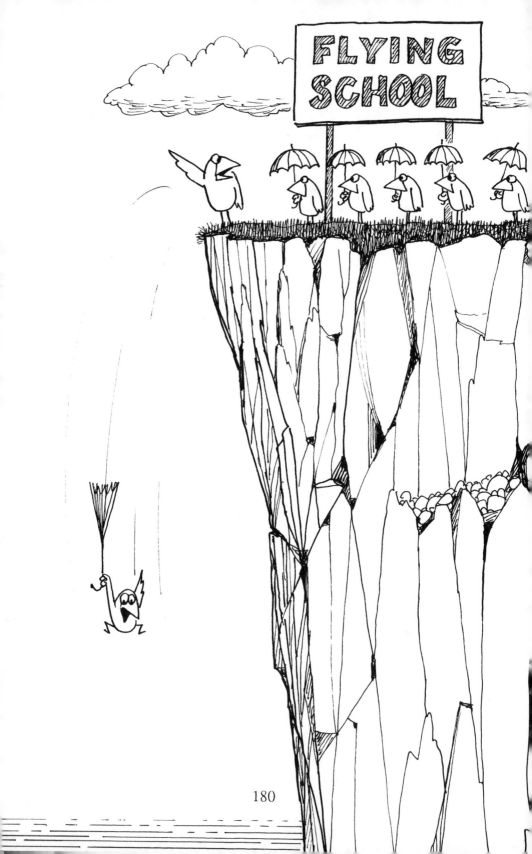

"*People are generally better persuaded by the reasons which they have themselves discovered than by those which have come into the minds of others.*"

Blaise Pascal

It is hard to give up evaluating others and start looking at ourselves. Yet, it is by far the most enlightening and effective type of assessment.

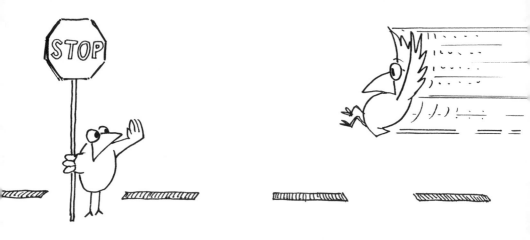

ROADBLOCKS TO SELF-EVALUATION

Roadblock 1: We are not used to asking these self-evaluation questions. Making these questions a part of our vocabulary is almost like learning a foreign language; it is a new way of thinking and doing. The ability to ask these hard questions of ourselves takes practice.

Roadblock 2: We are afraid that if we begin to rely less on evaluating kids, we will lose control of them (if we ever had any in the beginning). But when we attempt to control kids through our assessments of them, then we are using a coercive behavior which eventually destroys our relationships with kids. We tell kids what they have done wrong and expect that this will cause them to change their behaviors. When they still don't do as we expect, then we re-evaluate them. It becomes a frustrating cycle for both the kids and the adults. Even if the kids eventually do what the adults would like, there has been so much negative energy invested in the process, that no one is left very satisfied. On the other hand, teaching kids self-evaluation shifts the control and the responsibility back to where they belong, back to the kids. The energy spent on self-evaluation is constructive, efficient, and leads to positive change.

TEACHING KIDS SELF-EVALUATION

There is a growing number of helping adults who are successfully teaching the self-evaluation questions to their kids at home and at school.* Though it is not an easy skill to learn, it is an excellent tool for kids to use and will eventually become a positive habit. In the beginning, they will need guidance, but soon, they will GET IT! These questions are empowering, foster independence, and teach personal responsibility. Kids will learn how to access their quality world pictures at the highest level of perception and how to make these pictures a reality.

*For more information on Quality Schools, write the Quality School Training Program, Institute for Reality Therapy, 7301 Medical Center Drive, Suite 407, Canoga Park, CA 91307 or call (818)888-0688.

CHOOSING A NEW ATTITUDE

7

CHOOSING A NEW ATTITUDE

Helping kids help themselves is very different from the traditional method of telling kids what to do, when to do it, and how to do it. Eliminating coercive "help" and teaching about perceptions, the quality world, and self-evaluation takes a great amount of effort and looking inward.

BUT IF WE WANT TO HELP

IT IS THE BEST CHOICE

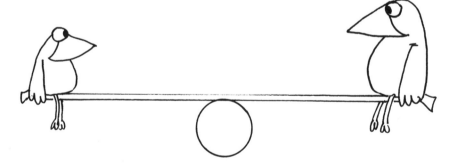

The ideas in this book applied one by one will help. But the net result of integrating these ideas into your life creates something bigger—it creates synergy.

WHAT IS
SYNERGY

TO PUT IT SIMPLY...

THE WHOLE IS BIGGER
THAN THE SUM OF ITS PARTS.

The synergy from these collective ideas sets into motion a new and creative process which both adults and kids can experience and explore together. When we keep our perceptual system in our awareness, when we focus on our quality world pictures at all levels of perception, we see things from the best possible vantage point.

OVERALL, WE CHOOSE A NEW ATTITUDE.

It is an attitude that redefines the traditional role that adults have played in the lives of kids.

THE NEW ATTITUDE

"We are equal. I am not above you. Let's get involved with each other. I want you to know the person I am, not just that I am your teacher, your parent, or your counselor. The best help I can give is being honest about myself, my life, and my beliefs. Then you have to make your own decisions."

It is an attitude which says that the only viewpoint a person can truly understand is her own. We see the world through the lens of our perceptual system.

THE NEW ATTITUDE

"You tell me how you see it, and I'll tell you how I see it. We can compromise and negotiate to reach an agreement. It doesn't always have to be my way, just because I am the adult."

It is an attitude that is based on the belief that people are internally motivated.

THE NEW ATTITUDE

"Tell me your hopes, your dreams, what you value, and we'll find a way to make them a reality. I know you will find your way, plus the determination to get there, if you know where you really want to go."

It is an attitude that says that self-evaluation is the most valuable form of evaluation.

THE NEW ATTITUDE

"As an adult in your life, my job is to be constantly evaluating MYSELF, not you. Your job is to learn how to evaluate YOURSELF, not me. If you need help, I am here for you."

Our role as adults in the lives of kids is to help them find their inner strength, their own self-love, and the dreams that will make their pursuit of long-term happiness well worth the effort.

There is within each of us
The strength to fly,
The love to support us,
And the dream to make
us try.

For many of us, adopting these attitudes will require a paradigm shift. This occurs when you experience a major shift in your perspectives or in how you view the world. A paradigm shift rarely strikes you like a flash of lightening.

The process usually occurs as a more gradual change in perceptions through your collective experiences, trials, and errors. Is it worth the effort?

Parents, teachers, and counselors spend a huge amount of time and energy trying to change their kids' behaviors and attempting to teach their versions of right and wrong. This approach leaves helping adults tired and unsatisfied after encounters with kids. As I go from homes to schools, I often notice that the adults look exhausted.

There is something terribly wrong with this picture. The problem is that the adults are taking RESPONSIBILITY for the kids' behaviors and long-term happiness. Are we helping kids when we do this for them? Absolutely not! Let's put the responsibility where it belongs—on the kids!

If kids do not learn how to be responsible for themselves and their actions, they will never reach independence. Our aim is to raise kids who can soar, who know where they want to go, and who have the insight and ingenuity to get there!

NO BIRD
SOARS TOO HIGH
IF HE SOARS
WITH HIS OWN WINGS
WILLIAM BLAKE

THE
END

(but it never really ends...)

Further Reading

Covey, Stephen R., *The Seven Habits of Highly Effective People.* New York: Simon and Schuster, 1989.

Glasser, William, *Reality Therapy.* New York: HarperCollins, 1969.

Glasser, William, *Control Theory: A New Explanation of How We Control Our Lives.* New York: HarperCollins, 1984.

Glasser, William, *The Quality School: Managing Students Without Coercion.* New York: HarperCollins, 1990.

Good, E. Perry, *In Pursuit of Happiness.* Chapel Hill: New View Publications, 1987.

Gossen, Diane Chelsom, *Restitution: Restructuring School Discipline.* Chapel Hill: New View Publications, 1992.

Pirsig, Robert M., *Zen and the Art of Motorcycle Maintenance: An Inquiry into Values.* New York: William Morrow and Company, Inc., 1974.

Simon, Sidney B., Leland W. Howe, and Howard Kirschenbaum, *Values Clarification: A Handbook of Practical Strategies for Teachers and Students.* Hadley, MA: Values Associates, 1978,

Sullo, Robert, *Teach Them To Be Happy.* Chapel Hill: New View Publications, 1989.

Wubbolding, Robert E., *Using Reality Therapy.* New York: HarperCollins, 1988.

Wubbolding, Robert E., *Understanding Reality Therapy.* New York: HarperCollins, 1991.

Beyond Further Reading
(The following books are theoretical in nature.)

Glasser, William, *Stations of the Mind.* New York: HarperCollins, 1981.

Powers, William T., *Behavior: The Control of Perception.* Chicago: Aldine Publishing Co., 1973.

About the Author & Illustrator

Writer E. Perry Good and artist Jeffrey Hale met 25 years ago while working at a San Francisco film studio.

Perry has taught disadvantaged youth, counseled runaways, and instructed mental health professionals who work with teenagers and adults. She received her Master's Degree in Educational Anthropology from New York University, then studied and worked with Dr. William Glasser, originator of the principles of Reality Therapy. Since then, Perry has become a noted counselor, theorist, and instructor in her own right. Today, she is a consultant and founding member of the International Association for Applied Control Theory. Her dynamic seminars are acclaimed by individuals, social service agencies, businesses, students, teachers, counselors, and other professionals. She lives in Chapel Hill, NC with her husband Fred Good, an artist, and their daughter, Jessica.

Internationally renowned animator Jeffrey Hale grew up in "Dreamland," the Coney Island of southern England. A graduate of the Royal College of Art in London, he has produced, directed, and animated numerous theatrical shorts, including "The Great Toy Robbery" and "Thank You Mask Man" (soundtrack by Lenny Bruce). His television credits include animation for commercials, specials, and *Sesame Street*, with which he has been associated since the show began. His work has been exhibited and honored at film festivals around the world and he has been nominated for two Academy Awards.

❖

new view
PUBLICATIONS

presents

Books by E. Perry Good

❖ *In Pursuit of Happiness*

New View's all-time best seller! Filled with humor and
amusing illustrations, this book explains basic human
motivation and behavior and provides easy-to-follow
exercises designed to help you become happier.

ISBN 0-944337-00-7

❖ *Helping Kids Help Themselves*

Perry explains that although we cannot force kids to be
reponsible and independent, we can help them move in
this direction. We can teach kids to self-evaluate what
they are doing and the overall direction their lives are
taking.

ISBN 0-944337-08-2

❖ *Overall Direction*

Perry offers a new way to help clients tap into their
quality world. Learn how overall direction questions
allow counselors to zero in on what their clients really
want. Both counselors and educators will appreciate
this powerful tool.

ISBN 0-944337-22-8

Call our toll free number to order these and other
New View titles, or to receive a free catalog...

1-800-441-3604

YOUR NOTES